Agnieszka and Włodek Bilińscy

POLAND

An Invitation to a Journey

text by Ryszard Bryzek

VIDEOGRAF II
Katowice

Małopolska
and the Carpathians

Silesia
and the Sudetes

Wielkopolska
and Kujawy

Mazovia

6

28

46

62

POLAND

78 Podlasie and Polesie

94 Warmia and Mazury

110 Pomerania

Introduction

Poland is a beautiful, interesting and varied country – read this and one may almost laugh at such an obvious, if not banal, truth. How often we tend to forget about her, dreaming about foreign trips instead, particularly to exotic countries. The current album is an accurate collection of passing impressions that present what is most precious in Poland. From the mountains towards the sea: the tour begins in the south, in Małopolska and its capital Cracow, the once-capital of Poland, which in its best times radiated its greatness almost all across Europe and today is regaining its past grandeur. Incomparable mountain landscapes, especially the Tatras, present one of the most distinguishing marks of this country. Passing through other landscapes, one can see castles and palaces of Lower Silesia – tracks of its rebellious history. In Wielkopolska, you may visit places where Polish statehood was born, in Mazovia you can brood among back roads and windswept willows, which were one of the sources of inspiration for Frederic Chopin. In Warmia and Mazury, amid thousands of picturesquely situated lakes, rise Teutonic Knights' castles and fortresses, which still recall the times of noble knighthood, great history and fierce battles. Finally, the seacoast offers relaxation in the famous spa resorts, amid golden beaches and rustling pinewoods. Apart from the commonly known attractions, you may sometimes encounter unusual objects, such as unique technological remains like the Augustowski and Elbląski Canals with their systems of ramps and culverts. On the eastern borders you may encounter Lithuanians and Byelorussians... and even Tartars.

The current album is not intended to be a comprehensive source of knowledge – it presents rather, as its title shows, an invitation to the versatile views of beauty of our mother country. It is orientated on what is most important, not on what is innovative, thus the reader is presented with places of interest having an obvious, undoubted value.

The castle in Pieskowa Skała

Podhale and the Tatras

Małopolska and the Carpathians

The territory of Małopolska (Polonia Minor) includes the water basin of the upper and central river called the Vistula. This name has been known since the 14th century and it was used in contrast to Wielkopolska (Polonia Maior), i. e. the territory, where the Polish state was founded. No doubt this is one of the most interesting, attractive, as well as varied regions of Poland. In 1978 Cracow was entered into the top UNESCO list of World Cultural and Natural Heritage, being at that time one of the twelve most valuable structures in the world, and moreover in 2000, the European Council awarded it the status of a European City of Culture. This is certainly one of the most beautiful cities in Europe. It is impossible to name all its precious monuments, as there are several thousands of them. Special attention should be devoted to Wawel Castle, which for centuries was the residence of the Polish kings and also the most significant centre of political power. The Cracow town square, which in the medieval times was the largest in Europe, is famous for the St. Mary's Church with its magnificent altar by Veit Stoss, and the beautiful Renaissance Sukiennice (Cloth Hall). Formerly, this was a place of cloth trade (hence its name). There are numerous charming houses, which are constantly being restored, as well as museums and galleries, unforgettable restaurants, cafeterias and clubs, which are nearly always crowded and full of life.

Wieliczka with its world-unique salt mine, the age of which is over 700 years, is very close to Cracow. Visiting the underground corridors and chambers gives you an idea of salt extraction in the Middle Ages. You can also admire statues made of salt, especially the precious figures and chandeliers in the chapel of St. Kinga, which is located 100 metres below ground.

Oświęcim, which lies in the neighbourhood of Cracow, holds one of the most horrible and fascinating monuments of mankind. Here in the concentration camps Auschwitz-Birkenau the Germans killed 1.5 million people during the Second World War.

The Cracow-Częstochowa Jurassic Rocks, a limestone area attracting rock climbers, especially in the summertime, reaches out from the north of Cracow through magnificent canyons of the Kobylańska and Będkowska Valleys. In the past, there were castles on many of the mountain peaks resembling eagles' nests. The whole chain of Jurassic-rock defensive castles originates from the Middle Ages and it was partly created by Casimir the Great. In the 17th century, these constructions lost their military importance and were easily captured and burnt down during the "Swedish Deluge". Today, they are romantic ruins adding a picturesque character to the landscape.

Located close to the beautiful Renaissance castle in Pieskowa Skała is the Ojcowski National Park, including the valley of Prądnik, which is the biggest and the most beautiful of all the Jurassic valleys, full of caves, rocky canyons, stone blocks, and foremost, the characteristic Hercules' Maul. The central part of the upland contains a natural curiosity, namely the Błędowska Desert – an inland region of moving sands and dunes, which unfortunately is continually being grown over by plants. The Cracow-Częstochowa Jurassic Rocks extend to Częstochowa, a town where a monastery is located on Jasna Góra, which is the most famous sanctuary of the Virgin Mary with its miraculous picture of the Black Madonna.

The Kielce and Sandomierz regions occupy the most northern part of Małopolska. These regions are most famous for the following valuable monuments: several Cistercian abbeys (namely the very well preserved abbey in Wąchock), castles and palaces (the palace of Cracow bishops in Kielce, the Mannerist palace of the Leszczyński family in Baranów Sandomierski), and above all, Sandomierz – the pearl of the Polish Renaissance, a town beautifully located on the steep bank of the Vistula, together with its Old Town, which is one the most beautiful in Poland. Here you can find a lot of monuments from the Old Polish Industrial Region, especially forging shops, furnaces and factories, reaching their top importance in the beginning of the 19th century, when iron ore was melted here and during the era of Stanisław Staszic and Ksawery Drucki-Lubecki.

Góry Świętokrzyskie (the Świętokrzyskie Mountains) are popular among witches, who fly at night on their brooms to Łysa Góra (Mount Łysa) to organise witches' Sabbaths here. In fact, the peak was in ancient times a place of a pagan cult and today it is also called Holy Cross, famous for its Benedictine abbey and church, which holds relics of the Holy Cross.

An aristocratic residence in Łańcut, surrounded by great gardens, possesses the biggest collection of carriages in Poland. Apart from this, there is the castle of the Lubomirski family, which towers above Nowy Wiśnicz, as well as a Mannerist castle in Krasiczyn.

The region of the Polish Carpathian Mountains includes only the northern tip of this huge mountain range, the most southerly parts belonging to central Romania. The genesis of the mountains goes back almost a hundred million years, when dinosaurs became extinct and the first mammals appeared on earth. At that time, one of the greatest geological movements in the history of our planet, called the Alpine Orogenesis, created a substantial part of today's highest mountains.

The main mountain group of the Carpathians in Poland are the Beskidy Mountains, which can be divided into the Western and Eastern Beskidy with their geographical border formed by the Łupkowska Pass. There is a substantial difference between the two mountain chains from the standpoints of nature, culture and economy. The western part is characterised by sharper peaks and steep slopes. Also its tourist infrastructure is better developed. Perhaps the Silesian Beskidy, located furthest to the west, a significant tourist region, especially for Upper Silesia, may be considered the most important. The "queen" of the Beskidy – Mount Babia (1725 m), which is several hundreds of metres higher than the neighbouring peaks, is famous for its incomparable panorama. A Carpathian primeval forest, covering most of the mountains, has survived almost untouched. Thanks to this, UNESCO among the World Biosphere Reserves lists the Babiogórski National Park. Many consider the Gorce one of the most beautiful mountain chains of the Beskidy for their vast peaks offering the most picturesque panoramic views. It is also possible to see in the old shepherd's sheep-cotes how they smoke *oscypek* (a sheep cheese) over fire. Very close to the Gorce you can find the Sądeckie Beskidy, which are famous for their various mineral springs. In their proximity, many spas were established; the biggest one in Krynica, as well as in Muszyna, Piwniczna and Szczawnica, where a kayaking route along the Dunajec breaks is a countrywide attraction. The rapidly flowing river intersects the "heart" of the Pieniny here and winds between lime slopes, which are often several hundreds of metres high.

To the east of the Łupkowska Pass, begins a region having shallow ridges and a few significant peaks. The eastern part of the Beskidy, of which we are speaking, is less populated and wilder. The Bieszczady and the Low Beskidy, which constitute a part of it, are characterised by small charming Orthodox churches, often hidden between small and abandoned villages. They are an integral part of the history, at times tragic, of the original inhabitants of this region, the Łemkowie. Similar to other Beskidy Mountain highlanders, as well as to the highlanders of the Tatra Mountains foothill regions, the Łemkowie are descendants of Wallachian shepherds, who came here in the 16th century along the Carpathian curve from the region presently called Transylvania and who mixed with the Poles from the lowlands. In the 1940's almost all their population was displaced from the Eastern Beskidy Mountains during the inglorious "Vistula Action".

The Tatra Mountains are without doubt the most exquisite, although a very small region of our Carpathian Mountains. These are unique Polish mountains with an Alpine character, which in their day, became very popular, and still are annually visited by herds of tourists. A real Alpine adventure is available in the high altitudes surrounded by rough nature and high dangerous canyons. At the bottom of the Tatra Mountains, Zakopane, the legendary town and mountain recreation centre is situated. In the course of its history, it has attracted numerous personalities, e. g. representatives of the Bohème, and significant personalities of art, culture and science. When talking about the Tatra Mountains and Zakopane we must not forget the original inhabitants as they have sustained the once rich culture. They are rightly considered the best of the Polish mountaineers. One of the best known elements of this culture is the so-called Zakopane style, introduced by Stanisław Witkiewicz, who designed several villas in Zakopane, drawing the patterns from mountain cottages. Among others, there are Koliba, Pod Jedlami and the chapel of Jaszczurówka. The characteristic feature of Carpathian flora is its stratified growth pattern. The bottom forest consists mainly of oak, pine spruce and fir trees, while the upper forest is dominated with pine spruce. Above the upper border of the forests, typical alpine vegetation begins, that is regions of Carpathian pines, then mountain pastures, and finally bare and rocky cliffs, which are located only in the Tatra Mountains, while Carpathian pines can also be found in the Babia Mountain range. The Tatras are in this respect exceptional, because some species, like Russian cedar and low cudweed, can only be seen here. The Tatra Mountains are also exceptional for their fauna – apart from common species living in the whole Carpathian Mountains like red deer, roe and wild pig, its territory is also inhabited by chamois, marmot and bear (which sometimes also visit the Żywieckie Beskidy and Bieszczady Mountains).

The Cloth Hall and the St. Mary's Church in Cracow

The Benedictine abbey in Tyniec on the River Vistula

The salt mine in Wieliczka – the Chapel of St. Kinga

The salt mine in Wieliczka – salt statues of a miner and the spirit Skarbek

The museum located in the former concentration camp, Auschwitz-Birkenau

The sanctuary on Jasna Góra in Częstochowa

The Hercules' Maul in the Ojcowski National Park

The castles on the Route of Eagles' Nests – Ogrodzieniec (A), Olsztyn (B)

Święty Krzyż – the Benedictine monastery in the Świętokrzyskie Mountains

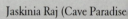

Jaskinia Raj (Cave Paradise

A 700-year-old oak tree, Bartek

The castle in Baranów Sandomierski

The castle in Łańcu[t]

Kazimierz Dolny on the River Vistula

The square and the Town Hall in Sandomierz

The Old Town in Przemyśl

The castle in Krasiczyn

An ancient Orthodox church in Smolnik, the Bieszczady Mountains

A bastioned Orthodox church in Posada Rybotycka

A sixteenth-century Orthodox church in Ulucz

A wooden church from the 15th century in Dębno Podhalańskie

The castle in Niedzica

The Tetmajer manor-house in Łopuszna

A highland cottage in Chochołów

An open-air museum in Zawoja

Połonina Caryńska – a mountain pasture in the Bieszczadzki National Park

On Mount Pilsko in Beskid Żywiecki

On Diablak Peak in the Babiogórski National Park

A ravine of the Dunajec River in the Pieniński National Park

Above Lake Morskie Oko
in the Tatras National Park

Silesia and the Sudetes

The present Lower Silesia (Dolny Śląsk) is to a great extent the result of the turbulent and complicated history in which it has been entangled. Until the 10th century, it belonged to Bohemia, then Poles took it over, ruling it until the 14th century when Czechs took it back again. From 1526 it was quickly Germanised, as it belonged to the Habsburgs, who lost this region in the 18th century in favour of Prussia. It was returned to Poland in 1945. At that time, all German inhabitants were relocated and the territory was settled by the inhabitants of eastern Poland. This complicated development of Silesia resulted in a mixture of different cultures. It is reflected in numerous highly attractive and interesting monuments, especially the impressive number of castles and palaces. The biggest of them is located in Książ, and together with its environs, part of which is a glamorous palm tree greenhouse in Lubiechów, they constitute the Książański Scenic Park. The superb castle, Czocha, originating from the 14th century, has been rebuilt several times, thus bearing traces of different styles. This is also the case of other great buildings in the region, many of which have Piast origin. Here are the most famous: the count's castle in Legnica, Grodno Castle in Zagórze Śląskie, Piast Castle in Bolków, and the castle of Oleśnica counts in Oleśnica. The turn of the 17th century, being a period of religious upheavals connected with the dominant position of Catholics and the persecution of Protestants brought over, apart from others, glaring Baroque monasteries and sanctuaries created by Cistercians and Jesuits. One of the most precious among them is the pearl of the Silesian Baroque – the Cistercian abbey in Krzeszów. Other Baroque monuments of similar importance include the Benedictine monastery in Legnickie Pole, especially charming due to the rainbow-coloured polychrome on the vault in its recently-restored interior, and the Cistercian abbey in the tiny town of Henryków.

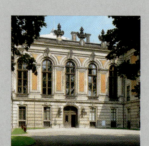

Wrocław, the capital of Lower Silesia, is situated on many islands bypassed by the Oder waters, and therefore, it is also called the town of one-hundred bridges, the oldest of which is the Sand Bridge (most Piaskowy) originating from 1845. The most renowned is the suspended Grunwaldzki Bridge. The town astonishes everyone by an incredible number of Gothic buildings, especially churches; the most significant being the cathedral of St. John the Baptist on Ostrów Tumski. Nevertheless, attention should also be paid to the monumental garrison church of St. Elisabeth, to the severe block of the Church of St. Mary Magdalene and to the huge church of St. Dorothy. The most magnificent Gothic building is the Town Hall surrounded by renovated houses on the square, the lace details of which evoke a fairy tale castle. The Baroque building of the Wrocław University contains a real jewel – Aula Leopoldina, full of paintings, sculptures, stuccos, wood-carving decorations and guilding. Away from the town centre, there is the vast Szczytnicki Park, dominated by the Folk Hall cupola, and nearby is one of the most interesting zoos in Poland.

There are several worth visiting tourist bases at the foot of the Karkonosze Mountains, such as Jelenia Góra, which is not only an excellent starting point but also the site of the Regional Museum with a beautiful collection of glassware; in Karpacz one should visit the church, which was transported from the Norwegian town Vang in the 19th century; and finally near Szklarska Poręba, there are two nice waterfalls, Szklarki and Kamieńczyk.

The eastern part of the Sudetes region is represented by the Kłodzko basin with the biggest number of Polish spas. The most famous ones are Kudowa Zdrój, Polanica Zdrój and Duszniki Zdrój, which are situated at the bottom of the Stołowe Mountains, where the magnificent and bizarre rock shapes attract as many visitors as the more famous Karkonosze Mountains. One can escape from such crowded regions to the far less visited

Sowie, Bystrzyckie and Orlickie Mountains, offering long walks along moderate and nearly deserted paths.

Upper Silesia is completely different. It is especially connected with industrial zones and characteristic pitheads of mines. Coal has been extracted here since the 18th century, which also resulted in the creation of a huge urban conglomerate of 14 towns, a feature not captivating at first glimpse. However, more careful penetration into the atmosphere of the countryside allows one both to perceive a particular attraction derived from the history of its hardworking people, and also perceive numerous historical and interesting places, including the housing estates of Katowice from the inter-war period, the Cistercian abbey in Rudy Raciborskie; the Black Trout Gallery in Tarnowskie Góry; or the amusement park in Chorzów. Woods form the surroundings of the urban expanse, where one can relax in the heart of nature. Lake Pławniowickie near Gliwice is one of such places. In the south area of the woods in Pszczyna, a noble palace surrounded by a beautiful park can be admired. The palace served as a hunting castle in the past. Today, an excellent museum is located there. In the nearby Pszczyńskie Woods there is a refuge which breeds bisons.

The Stołowe Mountains National Park – Szczeliniec Reserve

Wrocław – the Town Hall (A), houses on the Main Square (B)

The cathedral on Ostrów Tumski in Wrocław

A view from the castle tower on Ostrówek in Opole

The House at the Partridge Cage in Legnica

The basilica in Wambierzyce

The former Cistercian abbey in Lubiąż

The Town Hall in Jelenia Góra

An entrance gate to the castle in Brzeg

The Książ Castle

The Czocha Castle

A miner's housing estate in Katowice-Nikiszowiec

The church in the Cistercian abbey in Rudy Raciborskie

The castle in Głogówek

The eclectic palace in Moszna

A chapel in the sanctuary on Góra Św. Anny

The Black Trout adit in Tarnowskie Góry

The palace in Brynek

The palace in Pławniowice

The Vang sanctuary in Karpacz

The Karkonoski National Park – a shelter-home called Samotnia (A), a shelter-home on Szrenica (B)

The Szklarki waterfall

Wielkopolska and Kujawy

Wielkopolska (Polonia Maior) is connected with the beginning of the Polish state – there are many places in this region which recall the times of the early Piast dynasty members. Even as early as the 8th century BC, a settlement of Lusatian culture flourished in Biskupin, today belonging to the most interesting archeological preservations in Europe.

Gniezno is known as the first capital of the Polish state. The most significant historical monument of the town is the cathedral originating from the 10th century, where nearly all Polish rulers were crowned for almost 400 years. Special attention should be drawn to the Door of the Gniezno Cathedral (Drzwi Gnieźnieńskie), a jewel of Romanesque art, with its embossed scenes of the life and martyrdom of St. Adalbert.

The commencement of the Polish state is also reflected in the Piast Route, on which apart from Gniezno, you can see Ostrów Lednicki, where an ancient Polish settlement existed in the 7th century and was later known as the seat of Mieszko I, and finally, Kruszwica, a castle of the Goplanie tribe, mentioned in the Chronicles of Gaul the Anonymous. According to legend, it was here where rats ate Count Popiel II. In fact, it was the Myszka family that deprived him of his reign.

Poznań, today a centre of Wielkopolska, under the rule of Mieszko I was, apart from Gniezno, a residential castle. Today it is a significant business centre and the second-ranking banking centre following Warsaw, due to the inherited economy and the entrepreneurship of the inhabitants of Poznań. In fact, these features are characteristic of all the inhabitants of Wielkopolska. The Renaissance Town Hall shining on the Old Town square in Poznań, with houses of various colours, is considered to be one of the most beautiful in Europe. The tower's astronomical clock is famous for its fighting goats, which appear 12 times per day.

Rogalin near Poznań, which is famous for its rococo--classicist palace and decorated with a French-style garden, formerly belonged to the Raczyński family. It is one of the most precious jewels in Wielkopolska. The park surrounding the palace prides itself with oak trees out of which as many as 954 were designated as natural monuments – among them, the most notable ones are "Lech", "Czech", and "Rus". The splendid castle in Kórnik, built in the English Gothic style with an old arboretum next to the Romantic park, is considered one of the most beautiful in Poland. Of course, the list of castles and palaces of Wielkopolska does not contain only Rogalin and Kórnik; there are many others, which are not far beyond these. We can name, for instance, the Renaissance building in Gołuchów, which from an architectural standpoint, is very similar to the castles on the Loire; the late-Baroque palace in Rydzyna; a small larch-wood hunting palace of the Radziwiłł family in Antonin; and the classical palace in Śmiełów linked with Adam Mickiewicz.

The Konin district will surprise you by an attraction of a different type. On the right side of the Ślesin-to-Kleczew road, a monstrous crater of the surface lignite strip mine is visible, which is dozens of metres deep and several kilometres long. Licheń Stary, near Konin, has been famous since long ago as a pilgrimage destination with the miraculous picture of Our Lady of Licheń. Lately, it has gained even more popularity, especially thanks to the controversial basilica built with such great pomp that today it is the biggest church in Poland and the eleventh largest in the world.

Kalisz, the second biggest town of Wielkopolska, boasts the oldest written genealogy in Poland. In the year 150, Ptolemy, the geographer from Alexandria, located on the map a settlement called Calisia, situated on the Amber Route. At the turn of the 18th century, the surroundings of Leszno, which is situated west of Kalisz, were a location of the creative activity of Pompeo Ferrari, a significant Italian architect who designed and rebuilt many buildings. In Rydzyna, at the residential palace of the Leszczyński family, using an Italian style he linked this palace-and-park complex with the town. He helped to restore the burnt church of St. Nicholas in Leszno. He also designed the central nave of the Cistercian monastery in Ląd. However, it is the dome of the central part of the monastery church in Gostyń which is considered to be the best performance of Ferrari, with its 17-metre diameter, the biggest in Poland.

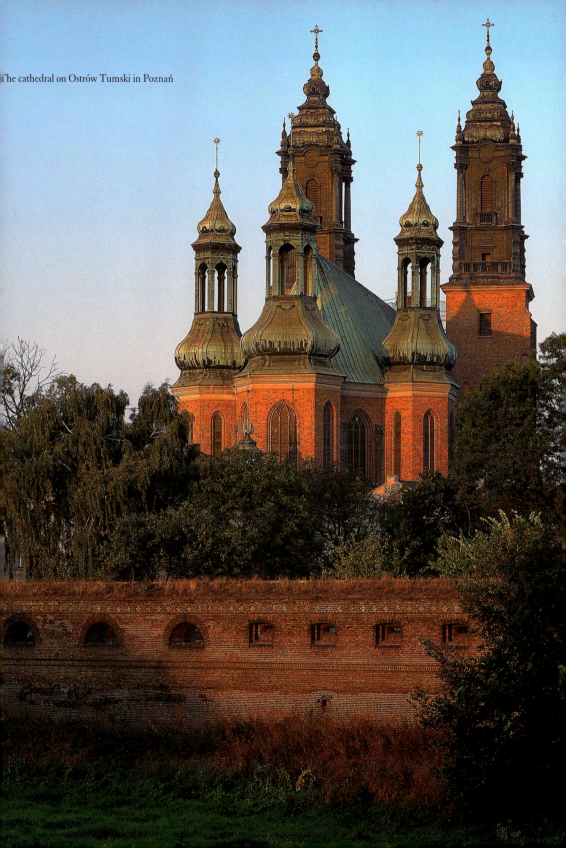
The cathedral on Ostrów Tumski in Poznań

On the Old Square in Poznań

Poznań – the parish church

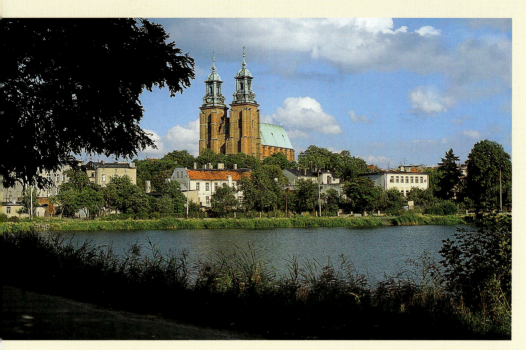
The cathedral in Gniezno

The Old Town in Kalisz

Toruń – a view from the Town Hall tower (A), Crooked Tower (Krzywa Wieża) (B)

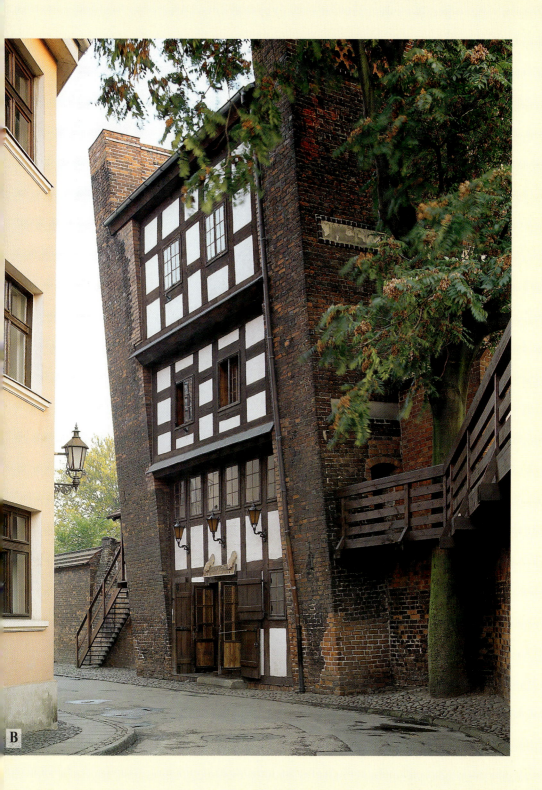

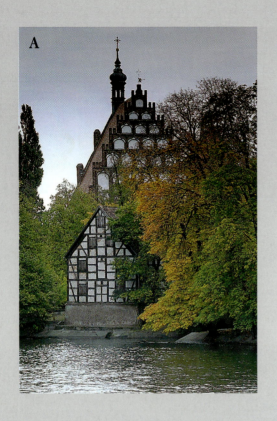

Bydgoszcz – the Church of St. Martin and St. Nicholas (A), on the Brda River (B)

The cathedral in Włocławek

A graduation tower in Ciechocinek

The Radziwiłł hunting lodge in Antonin

The castle in Gołuchów

The palace of the Poznań bishops in Ciążeń

The palace in Dąbrówka Wielkopolska

The palace in Winna Góra

The castle in Kórnik

The Ujście Warty National Park near Słońsk village

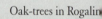
Oak-trees in Rogalin

The panorama of Łagowski Scenic Park from the castle in Łagów

Lake Gopło

In the Warta valley

Mazovia

This region, where the famous Pole Frederic Chopin was born, evokes thoughts about rural nature. In the lowlands prevail vast grasslands and farms cut by lanes of broad willows. The soil consists primarily of sand, which is the reason the forests are dominated by pine trees. Other trees to be seen here are oaks, hornbeams, birches and aspen. Willows and poplars grow in river valleys and somewhat further from the river banks there are ashes and elms. These remains of deep primeval forests, which used to grow all over the region in the Middle Ages, are also the dwelling grounds of some rare animal species such as the moose, lynx, badger, crane, black stork, and the moor buzzard. The Kampinoska Primeval Forest, often called the green lungs of the Polish capital, was declared a national park in the year 1959. The park's primary role is to protect its unique set of inland dunes and natural plant communities. Other parts of the primeval forests now consist of six scenic parks.

Occupying the central part of Mazovia, Warsaw is a city of a unique character. It is the most industrialized and the fastest developing city in Poland. The capital of our country has already become an important European city, but as one watches the ever-growing huge glass buildings, which are constructed next to the formerly unbeatable competitor, the Palace of Culture and Science, one gets the impression that the appetite to be a huge and modern centre is insatiable. In this new era, we are likely to forget that this city used to be an architectural achievement of the socialist realism, considered by some as a proud feature of national growth, and by others as coarse constructions deteriorating the city character. Luckily, the real architectural treasures are well-preserved even in this rush for greatness and the real pearls of the past are protected with reverence and consideration, the residuals of which were raised from decay by the inhabitants of Warsaw after the period when the fascist occupant made orders to blow away every house and construction in order to destroy everything. Therefore, today we can enjoy the Old Town and the Royal Castle in the same condition as they looked before the war, as well as Łazienki Park and Wilanów, and precious palaces and churches, the ruins of which were to be found all over the town. Just take a walk in Krakowskie Przedmieście or Nowy Świat and you will realise that Warsaw can be really elegant and interesting aside from its modernity.

South of Warsaw lies a plain where fertile soil and optimal climate helped the existence and development of one of the biggest fruit-growing regions in Poland and where the well-known Konstancin-Jeziorna spa is located.

Zelazowa Wola is a tiny but famous village which is visited by thousands of piano music enthusiasts every year. It was here that Frederic Chopin was born in the year 1810. His native house is today a biographical museum, where portraits of him and his family as well as historic furniture can be seen.

Among other jewels of Mazovia rank certainly Nieborów and Arkadia, owned in the 18th century by Michał and Helena Radziwiłł, great patrons of art who created a romantic palace/park complex. Many architectural details such as classical statues are hidden among thousands of trees and bushes, growing in apparent chaos around the beautiful pond in this park. Łowicz is located in nearby, distinguished by one of the most valuable urban sights in Mazovia. Chapels, which once stood by roads, are gathered in the Łowicz Museum, together with a splendid collection of traditional folk wear and patterned cut-paper art. But not only Łowicz is known for its folklore. Rich cultural items of the Kurpie people in the north of this region – coloured costumes, carts, traditional handmade products – can be admired not only in various indoor and outdoor museums, but also in the countryside during feasts and festive days.

Łódź lies on the border between Mazovia and Wielkopolska and it is known as the biggest centre of the textile dustry. However, the period of prosperity described, among others, by Władysław Reymont in his novel *Promised Land* is rather a part of history than reality. The heritage from this period includes, for instance, magnificent blocks of flats or factories and residences, which once belonged to German and Jewish businessmen. One of the most important residences is Księży Młyn, one of the biggest laundries of the past century in Europe. At the end of the 19th century and in the early years of the 20th century, it belonged to the 'king of cotton', Karol Scheibler. Many impressive blocks of flats run along Piotrowska Street, which is said to be the longest street in Poland. It is also an impressive centre of entertainment and social life with numerous elegant restaurants, noisy pubs, exclusive shops and street shows.

The Chopin's residence-museum in Żelazowa Wola

Warsaw

The Warsaw Mermaid on the square of the Old Town

Warsaw – a panorama view from the far bank
of the Vistula (A),
the Royal Castle (B),
the 'Palace on the Water' in Łazienki
Park (C),
the palace in Wilanów (D)

C

D

An Art Nouveau house in Piotrkowska Street in Łódź

The cathedral on Tumskie Hill in Płock

The castle in Pułtusk

A romantic park in Arkadia

The palace in Nieborów

The residence-museum of Jan Kochanowski in Czarnolas

The palace in Jabłonna

Ruins of the castle in Czersk

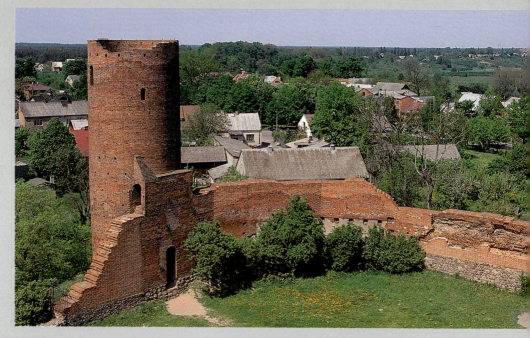

An Easter-Sunday morning service in Łowicz

Palm Sunday in the village of Łyse in the Kurpie region

A Mazovian farmhouse in Złaków Borowy

The Nadbużański Scenic Park

The Kampinoski National Park –
meadows at the village of Kępiaste (A),
Sieraków Reservation (B)

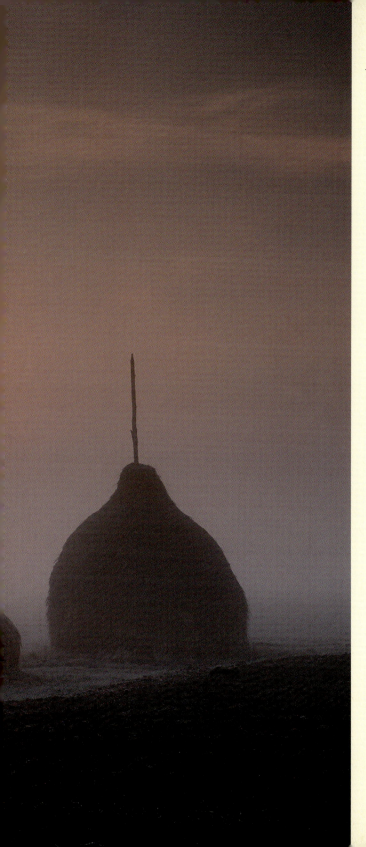

A dawn in Mazovia

Podlasie and Polesie

The intact nature, uninfluenced by civilisation, presents the greatest wealth of Podlasie, a weakly developed area with a small population density. It is protected in several national parks and reserves, and until now the area has been preserved from the touch of man's hand. The extraordinary value of the Białowieża National Park was recognized by UNESCO and entered in the list of biosphere reserves and also the world heritage list. The park contains Białowieża Primeval Forest, the intact old growth, and, in parts, primeval forest. This is the only forest of such large size and with such extraordinary wealth of flora and fauna in all of Europe. Only part of the park can be visited, and only with a guide. The greatest attraction is the bison – the symbol of the park and the biggest European mammal, which can be observed in the display reserve.

The largest in Poland is the Biebrzański National Park, an elk refuge, which contains wetlands and affluents to the Biebrza River, peatbogs and swamps, where a multitude of different birds can be seen, their lovers coming from almost all of Europe. Among others, visitors can also go to the Red Swamp Reserve, where the tourist can walk through thanks to wooden footpaths and bridges.

Among the historical sights in Podlasie, one should mention: the late-Baroque palace/park complex in Bialystok called the Versailles of Podlasie, the Baroque church of St. Trinity making the whole front of the town square in Tykocin, the Baroque palace with a park in Choroszcze (the summer residence of the Branicki family) and late-Gothic cathedral of St. Michael Archangel and St. John the Baptist in Łomża.

Various cultures and religions have met in Podlasie, sometimes very different. Catholic, Orthodox and Islam followers of various nationalities like Polish, Lithuanian, Byelorussian, and Tartar live here. Thanks to this fact, in Kruszyniany and Bohoniki we can see mosques built by Tartars to whom these villages were granted in 1679 by Jan III Sobieski for fighting on the Poles' side in battles against Turks. Their descendants live here up to this day, however, they have mixed with other inhabitants and they are no easily recognized. On Mount Grabarka, near a village of the same name, stands the most important Orthodo church in Poland, and moreover, a pilgrimage centre calle "the Częstochowa of the Orthodox Church." In Ha jnówka, "the gate" to the Białowieża Na tional Park, there is the largest co temporary Orthodox church, under th patronage of St. Trinity; it is regarded a one of the most interesting sacred build ings in the world.

Calm and undulating loess area stretch further to the south. There are no many cities in the Lublin region and th Polesie region – Lublin is the biggest cit It is underestimated to some extent, sti there are numerous beautiful sigh there. The Old Town itself, to which on goes through the Gothic-Baroque Cracow Gate (Bram Krakowska), has many cosy lanes. Outside the city centr the Neogothic facade of the castle is the main focus of a tention. The Holy Trinity Chapel, which is situated in th courtyard of the castle, is the most precious building i Lublin. In 1418, inside the chapel, Russian painters mad beautiful polychromy to Władysław Jagiełło's order.

The spirit of Renaissance is still present in Zamoś designed in the second half of 16th century by an outstand ing Italian architect Bernardo Morando to the order of Ja Zamoyski, a magnate and crown hetman of Poland, th founder and owner of Zamość. The urban complex wa built on the pentagon pattern and has a chessboard struc ture. It is so unique that in 1992 UNESCO placed it o The World Cultural and Nature Heritage List. Eac building is a world class sight. Obviously, the dominar style is Renaissance. The central and the most importar part is The Great Market (Rynek Wielki), surrounded b two-storeyed tenement houses, built according to one pa tern – their colourful facades are decorated with ornamen which bring to mind Oriental art. The Town Hall with it soaring clock tower dominates the marketplace, and i front stairs shaped like a fan are an unquestionable asset.

Votive crosses and the Orthodox church on Penitent Hill in Grabarka

The Branicki family palace in Białystok

Tykocin on the River Narew

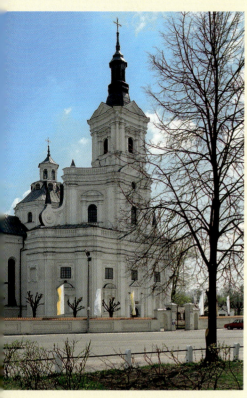
The sanctuary of the Virgin Mary in Kodeń

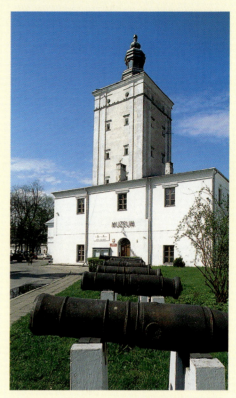
The castle complex in Biała Podlaska

Drohiczyn on the River Bug

A mosque in Kruszyniany

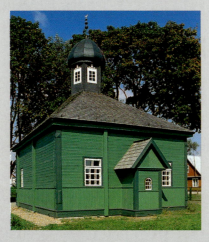

A mosque in Bohoniki

An interior of the Uniate Orthodox church in Kostomłoty

The conciliar Orthodox church in Bielsk Podlaski

The palace in Choroszcz

The Ossoliński family palace in Rudka

The open-air museum in Ciechanowiec

Arab horses in the horse-breeding farm in Janów Podlaski

The castle in Lublin

The Town Hall in Zamość

The chapel on the water in Zwierzyniec

The Zamoyski family palace in Kozłówka

Monumental oaks and village chapels in Górecko Kościelne

The Orthodox church in Radruż

The Białowieża Primeval Forest

The Biebrzański National Park

The Narwiański National Park

The Szumy nad Tanwią Reservation in the Solska Primeval Forest

The Scenic Park
'Podlaski Przełom Bugu'

Warmia and Mazury

In the early medieval times the territory of present-day Warmia and Mazury was settled by the Prussians. The Teutonic Order, brought to Poland in 1226 by Konrad Mazowiecki, was supposed to return the lands. The Teutonic Knights obtained the land of Chełmno, where they built their order state. Later they conquered the neighbouring Warmia region, which was annexed to Poland in 1406. Countless tracks of their reign are still visible even today. They founded many towns in these areas and also several castles. The most interesting can be found in Nidzica, Kętrzyn, Barciany, Ryn and ruins can be seen, for instance, in Ełk, Szczytno, Morąg or Szestno. The expansion of the order and capture of new territories led to war: one of the most important battles was that of Grunwald, in fact, it was one of the most important battles in Polish history. Today, a monument immortalizes this event, together with the Museum of the Battle in Grunwald.

The Church had a great influence here and that is why the sacred buildings are among the most invaluable sights. Attention is drawn to the marvellous cathedral in Frombork, where Nicholas Copernicus wrote his grand work *De revolutionibus orbium coelestium*. The bishops' seats were at one time very imposing castles. You can visit them in Lidzbark Warmiński, Reszel, Olsztyn, or Szymbark (ruins only). Much later, only in the 17th century, a church in Święta Lipka was built and it is one of the best known sanctuaries devoted to the cult of the Virgin Mary and a pearl of Baroque architecture. Historical landmarks here come from contemporary times: from the Second World War comes Wolf's Earthworks (Wilczy Szaniec), where Hitler's headquarters were situated. Even today the reinforced concrete walls, eight-metres thick, and the system of underground tunnels impress all who see them. Another attraction is the fortress Boyen in Giżycko, which, in the time of war, was the seat of the intelligence organization where spies were trained. Near Elbląg runs the Elbląski Canal, which is more than sixty kilometres long. For overcoming the change in height, with a difference of one-hundred metres, a system of ramps was built of a scale unique in Europe. The ships are placed on platforms that ride on tracks.

The rich nature of the Masurian Lake District is, to a certain extent, a result of the Baltic Sea formerly being iced over, which then carved out the troughs and basins of the lakes and left giant rocks (there is a collection of large rocks in the Fuledzki Róg nature reserve) and unique forms in the landscape, such as *kemy* – irregular hills with a calm slope, drumlins, repeated wavy hills and out washes – vast plains formed by the sand accumulated by water from the melting glaciers. Among the lakes, which are part of the Masurian Lake District, the Great Lakes Area enjoys the greatest and most deserved popularity. Especially yachtsmen love it: there is no other place in Poland where you can cross so many kilometres of vast spaces in your yacht – Lake Śniardwy is the biggest in Poland and it is difficult to see from one side to the other. There are also yacht clubs on the shores, which guarantee the right atmosphere. In such places as Mikołajki, Ruciane-Nida, Giżycko and Węgorzewo, which are also important places of tourism, you can listen to the chants and sailors songs at nights in the taverns and a walk on the quayside gives you the possibility to meet the sailor's world.

Glorious terrains of the glacial landscape, once grown over by a vast primeval forest, are left now with only some forest ecology.

One of the largest is the Piska Primeval Forest. Its tranquillity and wildness enchanted the eminent Polish poet Konstanty Ildefons Gałczyński. Towards the end of his life, he settled in a gamekeeper's lodge named Pranie on the shore of Lake Nidzkie, devoting many of his poems to the beauty of this nook.

Among the places of nature which are particularly worth a visit is Łuknajno Lake, with one of the large olonies of mute swans in Europe. The reserve, which surrounds the lake, was entered into UNESCO and it is now on the list of the world's biosphere reserves.

The Suwalskie region is generally considered to be an extension of Mazury, even though from a geological standpoint it is a part of the Lithuanian Lake Plain, which spreads even further east. A glacier has carved the land: blue lakes are hidden among picturesque moraine hills. Above the largest, Lake Wigry, there is a village of the same name and adjacent to it, on an island, a Camelolite abbey complex was built; its hermitage has been adapted into an enchanting resort centre. Lake Wigry is also a part of one of the most beautiful kayaking routes in Poland, as one follows the Czarna Hańcza River. When traveling along this route you can admire the beauty of the virgin Augustowska Primeval Forest and also visit an extraordinary and very interesting sight of engineering craftsmanship – the Augustowski Canal designed at the beginning of the 19th century by Ignacy Prądzyński, who also supervised its construction.

A Lithuanian minority is quite active in this region and thus, when visiting this region, you can, for example, taste Lithuanian cuisine specialties in many restaurants, among others blinas – tasty fried pancakes similar to flapjacks. The main seat of the Lithuanians is in Sejny. A local Baroque basilica of the Visitation of Our Lady has a beautiful rococo interior, which is regarded as one of the most precious sights of the Suwalskie region.

The Piska Primeval Forest

The castle in Olsztyn

The castle in Nidzica

The castle in Lidzbark Warmiński

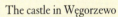

The castle in Węgorzewo

The castle of the Warmia bishops in Reszel

The palace in Sorkwity

An old windmill in Ryn

The sanctuary in Święta Lipka

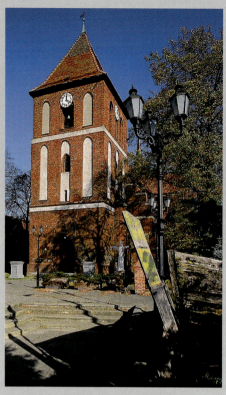
A church from the 14th century in Tolkmicko

The church of the Holy Cross in Braniewo

The Cathedral Hill in Frombork

On the route of the Ostróda-Elbląg Canal

The Walsza Ravine Reservation

Lake Jeziorak

Lake Jaczno
in the Suwalski Scenic Park

The Scenic Park of the Elbląg Highlands

The Mazurski Scenic Park – Lake Bełdany (A), the Krutynia River (B)

The Czarna Hańcza River

Lake Wigry

Pomerania

The greatest treasure of Pomerania is the Baltic seaside. The beaches covered with golden sand and isolated by stretches of dunes from one side and the sea on the other, attract every year large groups of enthusiasts who enjoy basking in the sun while listening to the gentle sea waves and calm draughts of sea breeze. Famous spa resorts offer not only sun and sea-bathing, but many of them also have precious sights and other attractions. Among the best known is Świnoujście with a stylish building dated from between the Wars, and Międzyzdroje situated nearby, where the biggest Polish film stars have recently left their prints in the pavement of Star Promenade. It is also a good base for trips to the Woliński National Park, which enchants you with its precipices up to one-hundred metres high and its deep ravines and pits. Here in the nature reserve it is possible to encounter bisons and the bald eagle, which is the symbol of the park.

The cathedral of St.John the Baptist, which towers over Kamień Pomorski, is one of the most important sightseeing attractions in Pomerania. Thanks to its monumental organs, every summer concerts may be heard here as part of the International Festival of Organ Music. To the west of Kamień Pomorski, Kamień Bay stretches further out with Chrząszczewska Island. On this island there is an unusual Royal Rock (Królewski Kamień), from which the name of the place and bay was derived. It is a rock with a diameter of about twenty metres. According to legend, the king Bolesław Krzywousty took the salute, as he stood here upon this rock, of the defeated Western Pomerania fleet.

One of the most interesting attractions of the bay is Trzęsacz. In the 15th century, at a distance of two kilometres from the sea coast, a brick church was built, although during the last two centuries the sea has eroded some parts of it and now all that remains is one fragment of the southern wall with two arch windows.

The biggest Polish spa is Kołobrzeg, where a once popular Festival of Soldier's Song has recently regained popularity. In addition to the basilica, lighthouse, salt beds, sanitariums, holiday houses and fish fries, there is also a small port – you can sail from it on a Viking boat trip or on Columbus' "Santa Maria" excursion ships stylised as historically reminescent sailboats. The regional centre of Western Pomerania is Szczecin situated at the Oder River. Even though it is more than sixty kilometres distant from the sea, it is one of Poland's largest trade ports, a town of water and greenery. The urban layout, based on Paris, comprises streets lined with trees radiating from plazas, the reason why the town once had the nickname "Paris of the North". Szczecin cannot boast of possessing a great number of sightseeing attractions for during World War II it was severely destructed. In spite of this, a majestic Renaissance castle belonging to the princes of Pomerania is worth a reference. The most representative avenue is Wały Chrobrego, with its colossal buildings and beautiful views of the Oder River. It brings one to the Maritime Museum, which displays interesting maritime collections and, among other vessels, an original Slavonic ship.

Pojezierze Myśliborskie, the lake district, which surrounds Szczecin and is not much visited by tourists, contains many spectacles – in Chojna there is one of the biggest sycamores in Poland, with a diameter of almost ten metres.

Situated inland, is Pojezierze Drawskie, another lake area, which is a sanctuary of nature unspoilt by civilisation. The forests here are full of mushrooms and fauna, the lakes and rivers abound in a great number of fish. Among the rivers, the most known is the Drawa, popular with canoeing enthusiasts; its middle section, which runs through the Drawieński National Park, flows swiftly through a deep carved valley, forming picturesque beaches. Floating down the river, you can have a look at Poland's largest military exercise field, if it is not in use, of course.

The one-thousand-year-old town of Gdańsk, the regional centre of Eastern Pomerania, is one of the three most important seaports in Poland. Many invaluable sights of historical interest come from an era of economic and cultural boom that took place between the 16th and 18th centuries. The most famous ones are situated along the Royal Road, traveled many centuries ago by Polish kings and merchants making their way down the amber trail to the trade port. There is the massive Renaissance Upland Gate (Brama Wyżynna). Right behind it, rise a torture chamber and prison tower. Passing by the terrace of the Golden Gate (Złota Brama) decorated with its statues, you enter Długa street, leading to the Town Hall tower and splendorous Arthur's Court (Dwór Artusa), where the facade draws attention to three big windows. The Neptune fountain in front of the court is one of the most distinguishing marks of the town. Apart from the Royal Road, Gdańsk gains interest also thanks to other attractions, such as the Old Crane (Stary Żuraw) and a granary on the Motława; the oldest church in the Old Town, St. Catherine's; the Cistercian abbey in Oliwa with its well-known organs (at the time of their origin, they were ranked among the largest in Europe); and also *The Judgement Day* – one of the most magnificent works by Hans Memling, which can be admired in the National Museum.

Sopot borders on Gdańsk, and is naturally connected with a wide, wooden pier, almost five-hundred metres long. In Opera Leśna a widely-known song festival is held annually.

On the eastern border of Pomerania rises a castle in Malbork, having an especially unique design in defensive architecture. It is one of its kind in Europe and has entered the UNESCO list of world cultural heritage. The fortress was the capital of the Teutonic Order state in the 14th and 15th centuries, and today it still wins interest, not only because of its dimension and architectural work, but being also the site of a museum having a glorious collection of products made of amber.

The Słowiński National Park has also entered UNESCO's list. It occupies the section of the Baltic seacoast with the coastal lakes, together with Lake Łebsko. Sand dunes there exhibit an unforgettable phenomenon. They are dozens of metres high and „travel" some distance annually, leaving behind a somewhat desolate landscape of dried-up tree stumps. Within the park's borders, there is an open-air museum in Kluki with a reconstruction of an old Slavonic village. The Kaszuby region makes up a substantial part of the territory of Eastern Pomerania. It is occupied by people of Slavic origin who, through hundreds of years of life here, have created their own culture, tradition, art and even language. The most distinguishing feature of their folklore is a flower pattern with a common tulip. Fabulously colourful embroideries decorate their clothes and fabrics, and the Kaszuby motifs are painted on their furniture, dishware, and, above all, ceramics. In Chmielno, the family line of the Necel has glued dishware for ten generations. You can visit their factory and observe how the famous ceramics are made. There is also a possibility to sit at the potter's wheel and then fire a piece of work in the kiln. In the oldest open-air museum in Wdzydze Kiszewskie, one can admire fully-decorated example buildings from Kaszuby: a school, a church from the 18th century and two windmills.

In the northern quiet and cosy seaside, are located the Jurata, Jastarnia, Chałupy and Hel resort areas, with clean and wide beaches, lined by a dune embankment and pine woods. It is a real paradise for those who wish to experience tranquil relaxation.

One of the most gorgeous areas of Kaszuby is Szwajcaria Kaszubska, a place of extraordinary geological variety, where the views evoke the atmosphere of the mountain terrains. The highest hill is Wieżyca, 331 metres above sea level. During the wintertime skiing takes place here. The lakes, in particular the Kółko Raduńskie, ten large lakes stretching along the Radunia River, enhance the quaintness. The forest, Bory Tucholskie, can be found more to the south, and it is a place full of bird life and game, and moreover, one of the largest forests in Poland. It contains nearby the village of Odra mysterious circles, which are remnants of the grave-mounds, and also the so-called "flat tombs", both dating back to the beginnings of our time.

The statue of Neptune in the back of the Artus' Court in Gdańsk

Gdańsk – a view on the Main Town from the other side of the Motława(A), Mariacka Street (B)

The organ in the cathedral in Oliwa

The pier in Sopot

The Nadmorski Scenic Park – a view of the Rozewie Cap

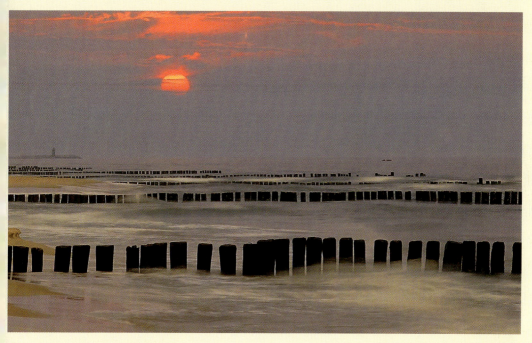

The sea coast in Chałupy on the Hel Peninsula

A storm on the sea

The Teutonic Knights' castle in Malbork

Houses on the square in Tczew

On the square in Gniew

The cathedral in Pelplin

The Wdzydzki Scenic Park

The open-air museum in Wdzydze Kiszewskie

Lake Raduńskie in the Szwajcaria Kaszubska region

The Forests of Tuchola

The Drawski Scenic Park

The Drawieński National Park

Lake Wisola
in the Iński Scenic Park

The Cedyński Scenic Park

The port in Kołobrzeg

Ruins of the church in Trzęsacz

The panorama from the lighthouse in Niechorze

Cutters on the coast in Międzyzdroje

Szczecin – a view of the harbour and Wały Chrobrego (A), the Old-Town Hall (B)

The Castle of Pomeranian Princes in Szczecin

The St. Mary's Church in Stargard Szczeciński

Layout and cover design
Anna Łoza-Dzidowska

Editing
Elżbieta Spadzińska-Żak

Typographical editing
Damian Walasek

DTP
Bogusław Trybus

Translation
Pygmalion – Czeski Cieszyn

2nd revised edition, July 2008

© Copyright by Videograf II, Katowice 2007
© Photos by Agnieszka and Włodek Bilińscy

Videograf II Sp. z o.o., Al. Harcerska 3 C, 41-500 Chorzów
tel.: (0-32) 348-31-33, 348-31-35
fax: (0-32) 348-31-25
office@videograf.pl
www.videograf.pl

ISBN 978-83-7183-613-8

Printed by:
Drukarnia Wydawnicza im. W.L. Anczyca S.A. w Krakowie